FAIRYTALE
BONES

Fairytale BONES

a collection of poetry and prose by

MICHELLE SCHAPER

300 SOUTH MEDIA GROUP

✦ ✦ ✦

NEW YORK

This book is presented as a collection.

ISBN-13: 978-1-957596-07-5

Author: Michelle Schaper
Book Design & Cover Design: Indie Author Solutions
Published by 300 South Media Group

TABLE OF CONTENTS

Halos and Horns   1
Hands of Time   2
Magical   3
Deep   4
Empress   5
Integrity   6
Kiss of Dawn   7
Shipwrecked   8
Poetic Sin   9
Passion   10
Fairytale Wings   11
Dynamic Emotions   12
Witchy Woman   13
Aesthetics   14
Fairytale Bones   15
Masterpiece   16
Wolf Heart   17
Emotional Energy   18
Lost   19
Heart Shivers   20
Musical Whispers   21
Gypsy Wish   22
Kaleidoscope   23
Ever After Poetry   24
Warrior of Love   25
Limitless   26
Soul Lovers   27
Enchanted Journey   28
Storm   29
Misfits   30

Whiskey Wolves 31
Sunsets Fire 32
Soul Song 33
Sleeping Beauty 34
Stop the Clock 35
A Mermaid Tale 36
Castles 37
Destiny 38
Masque 39
Snow White Bones 40
Glass of Heart 41
Melody 42
Once Upon a Wolf 43
Blossom 44
Butterflies and Lullabies 45
Dreams and Nightmares 46
Star 47
Heart Songs 48
Priceless 49
A Cinderella Story 50
Becoming 51
Kissing Melancholy 52
Heartbeats Kisses 53
Bleed 54
Unfuckwithable 55
Heart Strings 57
Lovers Kiss 58
Beauty with an Edge 59
Wolf Kiss 61
Dreaming 62
The Truth About Love 63
Wildheart 64
Phoenix 65
Senses of the Soul 66

Mettle Heart   67
Demons on my lips   68
Soldier   69
Nobility   70
The Little Mermaids Tears   71
Shield of Hope   72
Pearls of Poetry   73
Instinct   74
Never Ending Story   75
Gentle Men   76
Primitive Art   77
Kisses   78
Your Song   79
Empty Echoes   80
Rebel Elegance   81
A Fine Lady   82
Red Riding Hood   83
Beauty and the Beast   84
Senses Caressed   85
Weirdo   86
Kingdom   87
Bloom   88
Sweet Poetry   90
Rhythmic Art   91
Always My Happy Ever After   92
Fuck Cancer   93

Author's Note   94
About the Author   94

As always, for Chelsea and Tiana

"I always believed in magic and so I believe in you."

PROLOGUE

Sometimes, I'm intoxicated from the way I feel and I know only a few will understand this but it's almost as if the sun has set inside of me, leaving behind it's crimson romance glowing through my veins.

An autumnal aura surrounds me while my heart beats kisses to the ribs caging it's fire, but my remaining bones, oh, my bones are full of sensations my skin will never be deep enough to taste.

My eyes can't keep secrets of my qualities from everyone as they seek those who feel me with their souls. And everything most consider ordinary, burns me with such beauty.

—Michelle Schaper

"She is a warrior woman whose weapon is wisdom carrying a shield of truth and wearing her scars like the goddess she was born to be."

—Michelle Schaper

Michelle Schaper

Halos and Horns

She is a wildflower,
a rose
petals and thorns
poetry and prose
halo and horns
She is velvet
and sandpaper
no one's to own
She is a rebel
an angel
All soul and bone.

ₓ°. ꙮ °○∘°.°∘○° ꙫ .°ₓ

*"It fascinated me, the way she could
bleed and blossom at the same time."*

Michelle Schaper

Hands of Time

When there's a fire we call the fire brigade,
a wreck where someone's hurt,
an ambulance is called
and criminal activity calls for the police
but who do we call for the souls on fire,
wrecked minds and crimes of the heart?
Where are the sirens and rescue crews
when you're drowning in your own tears while
thoughts blaze through your mind stealing away
every happy notion,
when all you can hear
is the sound of your own heart breaking?
There is only hope.
Let it find you and seep through the cracks.
Let time cup your heart in its hands
and caress your mind;
And let the lips of life forever kiss your soul.

x°. ☺ °○₀°.°○○° ℂ .°x

*"It's time to stop hiding behind shadows of your heart
and step into the light from your soul."*

Michelle Schaper

MAGICAL

She found something magical
everywhere she went,
the girl who feels everything
I don't remember ever seeing her
without goosebumps
but I think she is the magic
and they were stars beneath her skin.

_x°. ꙮ °○∘°.°∘○° ꙍ .°_x

"(Soulbraille) -
Do you sometimes think that goosebumps could be braille upon our
skin? Words written from our souls of feelings hidden deep within."

DEEP

Look for me with your heart
Because I'll be somewhere deeper
than your eyes will see.

ₓ°. ᕲ °○∘°.°∘○° ℮ .°ₓ

"And though I love the way you look at me, won't you please see me with your heart. So when I've left your sight you'll still feel every beat of my beauty."

EMPRESS

She is an involuntary queen
battles lost with her own mind
forged scars into her skin
and tiny soldiers held the fort
around her heart for so long
But she has learned how to build entire empires
from all the ruins of her soul.

$_x°.\ \text{☾}\ °\text{○○}°.°\text{○○}°\ \text{☽}\ .°_x$

*"(Queen) – And she straightens every crease in her heart
like she's straightening her crown."*

Michelle Schaper

INTEGRITY

My soul has tasted heartache
my lips have kissed some shame
I have swallowed all my pride
and sipped upon some blame
I've nibbled at regret
I have craved a love that's true
I was force fed many lies
and bitten more than I could chew
I've had poems melt in my mouth
now I savour poetry
but nothing tastes so sweet
as the flavour of integrity.

x°. 🌙 °○∘°.°∘○° ☾ .°x

"Those who don't see your soul are the ones still searching for their own."

Michelle Schaper

KISS of DAWN

She was never just another
midnight mistake of his,
she put starlight in his eyes and made
his heart and soul feel sensations
he'd not known before
she went way beyond midnight
she was the kiss of dawn
stretching her bones over the sky
she was day kissing night
that first touch every time.

x°. 𝕯 °○°°.°○° 𝕰 .°x

*"Even the stars seemed to take a step backwards in
her presence or maybe the sky come forward to be
kissed by every beat of her heart."*

Michelle Schaper

SHIPWRECKED

We build boats out of our fears
then shipwreck our own hearts.

x°. 𝔾 °○°·.°○° ℓ .°x

"Be a little drop of love in someone's ocean of pain."

Michelle Schaper

POETIC SIN

And there she was somewhere
between heaven and hell
trapped in her circle shaped heart
not telling where the cracks
might end or begin
not knowing if she might be
the poet or the poetry
the sinner or the sin.

$_x$°. ☾ °○○°.°○○° ☾ .°$_x$

*"She wore her hell louder than the reddest lipstick
but left a little bit of heaven in every kiss."*

Michelle Schaper

PASSION

I don't want calm
I want intense
I want your breath to tear skin
from my flesh
I want the passion in your eyes
to burn me to the bone
I want the pure sight of me
to make your soul moan.

x°. ☽ °○○°.°○○° ☾ .°x

"She will love you so hard your heart will need a safe word."

Michelle Schaper

FAIRYTALE WINGS

She's just one of those beautiful creatures with
qualities deeper than desirable features
not made from sugar and spice
but a balance of light and dark things
if she were a fairytale character
she'd be a wolf with wings.

$_x$°. ☾ °○∘°.°∘○° ☽ .°$_x$

*"I always wondered how such a wild one like her could be so full of
nighttime things yet shine, like a thousand fiery suns."*

Michelle Schaper

DYNAMIC EMOTIONS

A sensitive soul
a heart of wild
you grew up thinking
you're a cursed child
embrace your blessing
it's not a curse
because you've been kissed
by the universe.

ₓ°. ☾ °○°°.°○° ☽ .°ₓ

*"The universe is sensually connected to her so she
embodies all life has to offer."*

Michelle Schaper

WITCHY WOMAN

Some say she's a witch of a woman
they don't understand the magic they feel
whenever they're in her presence
her dream – like aura gives a sense of surreal
she runs with the wolves and gypsies
they'll always have her back
she has a heart made of pure moonlight
but her soul is bohemian black.

x°. ☽ °o°°.°o° ☾ .°x

*"She is magic and mystery wears midnight like a dress
she's warrior witchy and a little bit princess."*

AESTHETICS

Beauty will always reduce me to tears
but I don't mean the visual kind
elderly stories of life in their years
the thoughts of a beautiful mind
The princess whose heart
beats for rock and roll
lines on faces
caused by outbursts of laughter
the misfit who dreams
with a patchwork quilt soul
the ones who put happy
into their ever after
the way some carry all of their pain
like a shield to protect many others
how everything softens
after a shower of rain
droplets of kisses upon lips of lovers.

$_x°. \, ☽ \, °\circ\circ°.°\circ\bigcirc° \, ☾ \, .°_x$

"When you love, everything you love is beautiful to you, the faces of people you love are especially beautiful but the true essence of beauty cannot be found upon a face it's what's beautiful inside of you that awakens all your senses."

Michelle Schaper

FAIRYTALE BONES

She looks like midnight
and her skin is fragranced with mystery
but she will breathe magic
into the stillness of your thoughts
awakening fairytale dreams
from echoes inside all the tiny spaces
between your bones.

$_x$°. ☾ °∘°˙.°∘○° ☽ .°$_x$

*"She was starlight within a storm from the tip of her toes and heaven
in a hurricane down to her fairytale bones."*

Michelle Schaper

MASTERPIECE

Tell me where you go
behind those hooded eyes
what makes your heart beat fast and slow
or causes heavy sighs?
Show me all your colours
in every different shade
the hues you keep a secret
in hope one day they'll fade
I'd like to know what stained your soul
who watermarked your heart?
So I can paint my love upon you
and together we'll be art.

x°. ☾ °○°·°○° ☽ .°x

*"Weave me into all the patterns of your thoughts and dream
of me in colours of your heart."*

Michelle Schaper

WOLF HEART

Her heart howling to the moon
for a love gone too soon
blinded by the call of lust
scattered now like midnight dust
A wolf heart hungry with desire
taste the burn, her soul on fire.

$_x$°. ☾ °○○°.°○○° ☾ .°$_x$

"She is a wolf and his heart is the moon her soul sings to."

EMOTIONAL ENERGY

Some say I'm an empath
light worker, healer
all I know, I am a 'feeler'
some say I'm a witch of a woman
for giving / feeling energy
all I know
ink flows through my veins
and my heart beats poetry.

x°. ☽ °○°°.°○° ☾ .°x

*"And even while you're sleeping my energy could
start fires in your dreams."*

Michelle Schaper

LOST

When you feel you've lost your way
and the walls of darkness seem too high
follow the light inside your heart
you'll soon see all the shadows fly.

ₓ°. ☽ °○∘°.°∘○° ☾ .°ₓ

"She would tear the stars from her own marrow on a clear night just to hang them in the sky to guide you home."

Michelle Schaper

HEART SHIVERS

Please, won't you forgive me
I'm at a loss for words
a song is trapped inside my heart
with butterflies the size of birds
all the musical sounds
make me catch my breath
while the lyrics are leaving words
shivering inside my chest
My spirit might have left my body
to go dancing down the street
but my heart,
my heart has met it's match
with each rhythmical beat.

ₓ°. ⑨ °○∘°.°∘○° ℃ .°ₓ

"I surrender to the seduction of music and fall in love with lyrics."

MUSICAL WHISPERS

She rarely ever sat still
always seemed to be moving
fidgeting, but lady like, you know?
I guess her body just couldn't resist
the sweet sounds of her soul
and the musical whispers
in the rhythm of her heartbeat.

$_x°.$ ☾ $°○○°.°○○°$ ☽ $.°_x$

*"But she could see dancing in all which was still and hear
music in all that is hushed."*

Michelle Schaper

GYPSY WISH

Sell me your soul in return for a kiss
you could be my gypsy wish
I'll sell you my dreams in lieu of a song
keep a piece of you in my heart
where you belong.

ₓ°. ☾ °○°.°○° ☽ .°ₓ

"Don't you come to me with a mouth full of promises and the taste of dreams upon your lips I want to run wild with your free spirit and feel nothing but soul within your kiss."

Michelle Schaper

KALEIDOSCOPE

She captures moments with her heart
to keep the memory of their beauty
she carries dreams and stories in her soul
with a pocketful of poetry.

ₓ°. ☾ °○○°.°○○° ☽ .°ₓ

*"She has the ability to look at life through a lens of
shattered dreams and still see love."*

EVER AFTER POETRY

Do you ache to touch my skin
or crave the thoughts of my heart
does your body lust for mine
or your soul fret while we're apart
do you desire the sweet taste
of my kiss upon your lips
or feel the rhythm of my heartbeat
in each swing of my hips
do you think of me
when listening to your favourite song
or whisper dreams inside your heart
of where we might belong
am I your breathless
flesh for fantasy
or ever after poetry?

ₓ°. ☾ °○○°.°○○° ☽ .°ₓ

"She hides stories behind her eyes, secrets inside her soul,
and poetry in all the places she wants to be kissed."

WARRIOR of LOVE

Do not mistake
her gentleness for weakness
or her timeless grace for vulnerability
she has pulled broken arrows
from her own heart
and used their sharp edges to carve a path
straight into a new dawn
while bleeding her dreams to life.

$x^{\circ} \cdot \mathcal{D} \; ^{\circ}o \circ ^{\circ} \cdot ^{\circ} \circ o^{\circ} \; \mathcal{C} \cdot ^{\circ}x$

"She is a warrior who stands up for her beliefs yet she is sensitive and has empathy for others and their griefs despite the tragedy of her own life she remains compassionate she likes simplicity but is forever passionate."

Michelle Schaper

LIMITLESS

It is my journey
It's only me
who can define
and set a boundary
but when it comes to passion
the places my heart loves the best
you'll find no boundaries
my soul will be limitless.

ₓ°. ꙮ °○°°.°○° ꙮ .°ₓ

"She stretches her bones across maps in her mind, places flowers in her hair and fallen stars in the pockets of her heart."

Michelle Schaper

SOUL LOVERS

I don't want to make love
I want to rub my soul
up against yours
and watch love
make us.

ₓ°. ♊ °○°·.°○° ☽ .°ₓ

"I want to hold you Like the sky holds the stars."

Michelle Schaper

Enchanted Journey

One night while I lay sleeping
I heard a dreams echo
I sat up upon my bed and decided to follow
I tiptoed to enchantment within a fairytale
climbed aboard a paper boat
began my journey setting sail
Before too long I met my siren soul
somewhat lost at sea
she whispered me a song
of shipwrecked poetry
on land again I found
a field of flowers, green and gold
I ran through the tall grass
listening to secrets being told
'twas there I laughed and played
alongside my inner child
she took me to the forest
to meet my heart of wild
Face to face with my own heart
I came to know my truth
I met all my worth in the full moon
and my loyalty, the wolf
So there was no fairytale
whispering a dream to me
was just my heart and soul
setting my mind free.

x˚. ☽ ˚o∘˚.˚∘o˚ ☾ .˚ₓ

"She is part child full of wild but all lady with soul."

Michelle Schaper

STORM

He has a dark enchantment,
demonic charm
but he is shell-shocked
by her lashes
she is wildfire, in a storm
when she blinks
lightning crashes.

ₓ°. 𝕯 °○∘°.°∘○° ℰ .°ₓ

"Thunder happens sometimes when there isn't any rain her smile is soft and calm but her heart beats a hurricane."

Michelle Schaper

MISFITS

Anyone can be attracted to obvious beauty
the visually stimulating
but me, ah,
I'm drawn to the misfits
the ones whose scars tell stories
who have patchwork hearts
and hand – me – down souls.

$_x°. \, \mathfrak{I} \, °\circ\circ°.°\circ\circ° \, \mathfrak{C} . °_x$

"The prince was never charming I found beauty in the beast."

Michelle Schaper

WHISKEY WOLVES

Be careful of her enticing kiss
there's primal instinct on her lips
and when she gently lets them part
you'll glimpse the wolf inside her heart.

x°. ꒰ °○°°.°○° ꒱ . °x

*"Sometimes the wolf inside my heart burns my chest and throat until
my moon appears so I can taste the sweet honey of my howling."*

Michelle Schaper

SUNSETS FIRE

She was just one of destiny's children
fighting her way through life
to get to the love
but my god, how she glowed,
like an angel
dipped in the dust of sunsets fire.

x°. ☽ °o∘°.°∘o° ☾ .°x

*"I will create my own sunshine and if its touch may
burn me a fire I shall be."*

Michelle Schaper

SOUL SONG

Although I love the way you look
and hear music
in your every exhaled breath
it's your soul has charmed me more
and all which sings beneath your flesh.

ₓ. 𝄞 °○°°.°○° ℮ .°ₓ

*"The only home I've ever known is a song buried
in blood and bone."*

Michelle Schaper

SLEEPING BEAUTY

She lays down upon a bed of self worth
putting her insecurities to rest
wraps herself in a blanket of hope
while sounds of dreaming
whisper through her chest
as she closes her eyes to the years
of self doubt she has known
her eyelids hide all the shame she's ever felt
and those words she once
told her reflection
sway on the tip of her tongue
as they now melt
she finally understands
the meaning of beautiful
in its each and every part
she knows the truest form of beauty
sleeps inside her heart.

ₓ°. ☽ °○∘°.°∘○° ☾ .°ₓ

*"I stopped looking for my worth in others, I found my worth in myself
and now only look for those worthy of me."*

Michelle Schaper

STOP the CLOCK

Sunshine won't lose power
and the trees won't run away
time will still pass hour by hour
if the clocks stop for a day
moonlight doesn't need downloading
flowers don't cut you off or overtake
and sometimes stars will shoot or fall
but they won't ever break.

x°. ☾ °○○°.°○○° ☽ .°x

"Listen for music in the sunrise and a heartbeat in every flower."

Michelle Schaper

A MERMAID TALE

My siren soul knows secrets
I carry in my spine
deep as any ocean
swimming in this heart of mine
my body is just a shell
holding stories, out of breath
you'll hear sounds of the sea
if you lay your head upon my chest.

ₓ°. 🌙 °○∘°.°∘○° ☾ .°ₓ

"She has the soul of a siren And a shipwrecked heart."

Michelle Schaper

CASTLES

We build castles in the air
Of hopes and dreams for you and me
Then dance in them like kings and queens
Wearing crowns of poetry.

x°. ☾ °o°°.°°o° ☽ .°x

"We make love More than we make sense And daydreams dance inside our heads."

Michelle Schaper

DESTINY

Destiny calls softly from behind
a heavy door inside my heart
she glances around at the crumbling walls
and makes no regard for the chambers there
filled with excuses
she carries on with her duties
dusting anything standing in her way
Destiny shines through
the darkest corners of my heart
guiding my soul and I
to all the places she's hand picked
for us to see
occasionally she is charming
but often she's stubborn
and she always wants to be the leader.

$_x$°. ☾ °○○°.°○○° ☽ . °$_x$

"Her rebel heart sometimes rewrites her own story, turning what's written in the stardust into ink and poetry."

Michelle Schaper

MASQUE

Some mistake
her shield of truth and protection
for a mask
but there is no lie in her light
just her heart
wearing an armoured casque.

x°. ☽ °○°˚.˚°○° ☾ .°x

"Fuck whatever mask you wear for the world show me your soul."

Michelle Schaper

SNOW WHITE BONES

She was the prettiest wild
you'll have ever seen
hair darker than night
flowing like a stream
moonlit skin softer
than a baby's breath
mountains moving with each
rise and fall of her chest
crimson rosebud lips
kissing you with a smile
though she had known darkness
for a little while
she no longer denies
her power within
her heart's beating stars through the skies
from her light within
Her snow-white bones had been set
from liquid moonlight
and her soul will forever
be shining so bright.

x°. ☽ °○∘°.°∘○° ☾ .°x

*"She is whimsically connected to the universe and wears
her wild like a princess dress."*

Michelle Schaper

GLASS of HEART

Pull up a chair
I'll pour you a glass of my heart
take sips of the warmth
past each jagged edge part
and when you are finished
let it settle a while
feel my hearts elixir
bring your soul a smile
then you can decide
if poison or antidote
the love in my heart
that burns in your throat.

ₓ°. ☽ °○₀°.°₀○° ☾ .°ₓ

"I took shots of your heartbeat and got drunk on your love."

MELODY

Your breath upon my skin
feels like poetry to me
caressing all my senses
a glimpse of ecstasy
your whispered words like dreaming
dripping from your mouth
intoxicate my heartbeat
like a sin that's not allowed
The touching of your fingertips
play me like a melody
the echoing of our souls
making sounds so sweet.

ₓ°. ꩷ °○₀°.°₀○° ℭ .°ₓ

"I have a fetish for heartbeats and the sounds of love they play."

Michelle Schaper

ONCE UPON a WOLF

Once upon a heart of wild
there lived an old soul gypsy child
ancient beauty through and through
believe her magic
she's the wolf in you.

ₓ°. ☾ °○∘°.°∘○° ☽ .°ₓ

"She's made of simple things that mean so much like flowers, smiles and truths sunshine and kisses, music, stardust, moonlight, raindrops, wolves."

Michelle Schaper

BLOSSOM

Pain took root deep down in my heart
grew twigs and branches
through my every other part
made its way inside my veins,
left me full of dirty stains,
turning my mind into a prisoner of the past
but the hands of time tenderly
caressed my soul
now I know the fingerprints of pain
helped me to grow
You will see new buds sprouting
there throughout my heart
bleeding all my hurts into a form of art
I'll keep my pain to remind myself I'm freed
for I will be blossoming
every time I bleed.

x°. ☾ °o∘°.°∘O° ☽ .°x

*"If you want to touch the velvet petals of her heart
you'll need to feel the bleeding thorns of her soul."*

Michelle Schaper

BUTTERFLIES and LULLABIES

Her butterfly heart
loves deeper than any ocean
And her soul
Sings a sirens song.

$_x$°. ☾ °○○°.°○○° ☽ .°$_x$

*"Sing me a song of saltwater kisses and dream me
a story from the sea."*

Michelle Schaper

DREAMS and NIGHTMARES

I remember things
I have not experienced
and I've experienced things
I don't want to remember.

$_x$°. ☾ °○°°.°○° ☾ .°$_x$

*"My soul seemed to remember when my heart first greeted you
our very first meeting was my favourite dëjävu."*

Michelle Schaper

STAR

When words fall from her pretty mouth
tumbling to your heart
it's as though she crawls
inside your chest
tearing your ribcage wide apart
she cups your heart gently in her hands
to feel your heartbeat kiss her palms
then settles in your spine
like a shooting star
arriving home.

$$_{x}°. \; ℑ \; °O∘°.°∘O° \; ℓ .°_{x}$$

"She was so delicate yet bursting with energy
kind of like a shattered star."

Michelle Schaper

HEART SONGS

That part, in a song,
the bridge or final chorus key change
of a power ballad
the bit that takes you to a new level
and seems to rip your heart from your chest
leaving it to float in your dizzy mind
I like the intoxicating feeling,
I like the tiny bubbles of skin
dancing along my arms and the lump
it brings to the back of my throat
that bobs up and down
not knowing where to go.
I like to feel my heartbeat synchronise
to sounds of the drums
and I like how my soul is soothed
when music becomes magic
the only thing I like more?
the people I love who make me feel
this way, each a different tune
they are the songs of my heart.

x°. ☉ °○∘°.°∘○° ☾ .°x

"I want your heartbeat on my playlist."

Michelle Schaper

PRICELESS

I wonder how anyone decides
on somethings value
a piece of gold or a vintage car
I don't understand this equity
show me a heart of gold,
because your smile is what's priceless to me
and that one teardrop glistening
upon your cheek
shines brighter and holds more worth
than any diamond or antique.

x°. ☉ °○°°.°○° ℮ .°x

"And when she cried she looked like an angel scattering pearls."

Michelle Schaper

A CINDERELLA STORY

Her heart is a carriage
drawn by the wild of her soul
it has never known midnight
as implied by the stories once told
she looks for life experiences
bringing inspiration and energy
romancing her own soul
while chasing her dreams
She falls in love with free spirits
who will never be tame
wildfire burns through their blood,
glowing cinders remain
When they get together they find
passion, kindness and courage
allowing each other the freedom
their hearts need to flourish
They nurture individual needs for affection
wearing crowns of intensity
then waltz together
like the princes and princesses
they were born to be.

x°. ☾ °○∘°.°∘○° ☽ .°x

*"She dances to the rhythm of her own heartbeat leaving
footprints across the sky while stumbling on stars."*

Michelle Schaper

BECOMING

I am calmly spiritual
with a natural quietness
giving an air of mystery
while nature is mostly a muse
for the poetess in my heart
my soul sometimes speaks
in a language of ancient beauty
My truth flows freely through my veins
thoughts come and go
so my sanity remains
I won't allow negativity
to leave seeds of doubt
with creeping shoots
embedded in my heart
you'll find integrity has roots
Succulent stems form branches into wings
So I can fly far from denial
way above the facade of all
who try to hang without a trial.

x°. ☾ °○○°.°○○° ☽ .°x

*"But you see, those wounds left behind from stabbings to my back
finally become deep enough for my wings to grow through."*

Michelle Schaper

KISSING MELANCHOLY

She took sadness as a lover
while melancholic kisses
caressed her thoughts
even darkness ran for cover
when her madness run its course.

x°. ☾ °○°°.°○° ☽ .°x

*"When pain demands to be tasted fill your cup until it's
overflowing then drink to know you're alive."*

Michelle Schaper

HEARTBEAT KISSES

Love felt like fresh linen sheets
a summer breeze, rosy cheeks
and buckling knees
love feels like home
wherever you may be
like fluffy clouds, long drives
and poetry
Love felt like a burning
through my chest,
like something stole away
all of my breath
love feels like a heartbeats kiss
a shooting star and birthday wish.

x°. 𝄞 °○∘°.°∘○° ℮ .°x

*"Let me lay my head upon your chest
to feel your heartbeat kiss my cheek."*

BLEED

Handle her heart with care
not because it's fragile
because it has sharp edges
from all the broken pieces
but if you're not afraid
to bleed a little
you'll find unlimited softness deep inside.

x°. ʘ °○∘°.°∘○° ℓ .°x

"She'll love you so softly it will hit you hard."

Michelle Schaper

Unfuckwithable

Her mind was not unlike a feather
with a quill made out of steel
light and airy to tickle your fancy
yet strong enough to keep it real
possessing cognisance which
she kept hidden for the most
this angelic intellect
wasn't ever one to boast
when faced with behaviour
from those with bad intent behind their eyes
she knew not to label the person(s)
or to conceptualise
this way she stays detached
from an aversion that could
cause her pain
so she'll rack it up as a lesson
which will only bring her gain
she'll sit with her sensations
and the way it makes her feel
and watch this experience
undermining attachment, so she can deal
She won't allow reinforcement
towards the way she's being treated
once again the strength of her mind
will not be defeated

continued

So she'll honour all her feelings
without falling for a conceptual trap
you will find she'll always be
Unfuckwithable like that!

$_x$°. ☉ °○○°.°○○° ℰ .°$_x$

"Unfuckwithable"

[un-fuck-with-able]

(adj) *when you are truly at peace*
And in touch with yourself,
And nothing anyone says or does
Can bother you,
And no negativity can touch you."

Michelle Schaper

HEART STRINGS

I think the whole world
is the spine of something bigger
and we are but the little bones
holding it together
we need to make connections
so it doesn't fall apart
or maybe we are the strings
and the whole world
is a pulsing heart.

$_x°.$ 𝕽 $°○○°.°○○°$ 𝖊 $.°_x$

*"She only has two small hands so she carries
the weight of the world in her heart."*

Michelle Schaper

LOVER'S KISS

Once upon a lover's kiss
you whispered dreams against my lips
you ran your fingertips
throughout my soul
as your heart beat the words
your voice never told.

ₓ°. ꩜ °○°°.°○° ꩜ .°ₓ

"I want to keep you like a secret and love you like a sin."

Michelle Schaper

BEAUTY WITH AN EDGE

She always liked the edges the best
she wanted to reach for borders
of clouds and the pretty shapes
they made in the sky
Details, oh how she loved
the tiny details
she liked to run her fingertips
along the edge of everything
she doesn't care for perfectly
straightened teeth or unblemished skin
she wants to see the stains
feel the bumps
she likes intrinsic patterns
to take root in her heart,
become entangled in her soul,
and she will intricately curl herself around
every beat of your heart
while counting blades of grass
by each pointy perimeter
She thought corners of stars
always seemed to soften
the darkness of night
and she kept her favourite things
in the contours of her lips
so they'd blend into

continued

the edges of her every smile
That's what gave her beauty
an edge of its own,
all the frayed sides of her heart
were smoothed by the magic
she found in the little details
in all of life's simplicities.

ₓ°. ୭ °○₀°.°₀○° ୧ .°ₓ

*"The sky is but a whisper of blue dreaming and clouds
are its every heartbeat."*

Michelle Schaper

WOLF KISS

The words falling from his mouth
have no significance to me
for even when we are apart
I listen to his spirit speak
what matters to my heart
are all the sounds of his souls truth
and the taste of his mouth
the kiss of a wolf.

$_x°.$ ☾ $°○○°.°○○°$ ☽ $.°_x$

"Oh how his lips taste like love."

Michelle Schaper

DREAMING

Time for me to go to bed
sleep doesn't come easily
how nice it would be to switch off my head
lock my thoughts away with a key
I wonder where my dreams will take me
I hope to an enchanted place
my pillow is soft and inviting
but my hair starts to tickle my face
Too many distractions now
as the sheet caresses my skin
my thoughts take me to you somehow
now a butterfly dances within
my thinking just won't go away
thoughts ripple like stones thrown at a lake
sleeping is overrated anyway
my best dreaming occurs
when I'm awake.

x°. ☾ °○°°.°○° ☽ .°x

*"I sleep with your name upon my lips when I open my mouth
the butterflies you gave me will be free."*

Michelle Schaper

THE TRUTH ABOUT LOVE

All of loves truths
are yet to be revealed to my heart
I think what is true
must be hidden in the relations
we find between mysteries
because love is immortal
and will forever intrigue
even the most stubborn of hearts.

$_x°. \, ☾ \, °○○°.°○○° \, ☽ \,.°_x$

*"I keep love with me in the strands of my hair the tips of
my fingers and my face as it turns to feel the warmth
of the sun. Love is a touch a taste, a favourite song,
I believe love is a feeling and a state of mind."*

WILDHEART

She is not afraid of the fall
her tenderness
is no sign of weakness
darling, crash through her heart
wall by wall
what you find there
could leave you speechless
she wraps her arms
around fear everyday
and sleeps next to the edge
of her fears
but what she's found in life
all the way
each form of love is worth all the tears
So show her how hard your heart beats
when she gives you
those thoughts from her soul
don't tame the wild in her heart
or under the sheets
and she'll love you hard
'til it's your turn to go.

_x°. ☾ °○°°.°○○° ☽ .°_x

"Her spirit is free she has a rebel soul but she loves
with all the wild of her heart."

Michelle Schaper

PHOENIX

Life has sharpened
its teeth on her heart
and left bite marks
in her soul
ripped her apart
swallowed her whole
still, she will rise
still, she flies.

ₓ˚. 𝄞 ˚○∘˚.˚∘○˚ ℓ .˚ₓ

*"She might have been put through hell
but she came back with a heart that beats fire."*

Michelle Schaper

SENSES of the SOUL

Sometimes I can feel vibrations
of my heartbeat
in all the little spaces
between my bones
the feeling can change
from likeness of a cat purring
to an engine humming in an instant
while my heart itself is a garden
throbbing with life, blossoming
I can feel each petal falling
and every root take hold
to something deeper inside of me
I don't know what could be more deep
beneath my skin and flesh than my heart
but it's there, I feel it
I breathe it.

x˚. ☽ ˚∘˚.˚∘◯˚ ☾ .˚x

"I feel things somewhere deeper than my body, than my mind
someplace my heart has seen somewhere my minds eye tries to
find my spirit has felt sensations my body has never known way
beyond sight and sound senses deep down to the bone."

Michelle Schaper

METTLE HEART

Her soul was flowered rose purple
like wild geranium
but her heart had long ago
been turned into titanium
she kept her values high
like a sturdy stiletto heel
and wore her metal heart proud
like a crown made out of steel.

x° . ☾ °○°°.°○° ☾ .°x

*"She is made from determination and resilience courage
runs throughout her veins and if you're fortunate enough
to have known her, you'll know she's the 'she' those
poets always write about."*

Michelle Schaper

DEMONS ON MY LIPS

I'm not like other girls
I live in many different worlds
where my soul likes to dance
and given half the chance
I'd be dancing in the rain
to wash away the pain
But this you already know
I won't say I told you so
'cause you saw something
in my eyes
that won't resemble lies
When you caressed
my mouth with yours
you had a taste
of all my flaws
The demons on my lips
drank you up in little sips
so now you swim inside my veins
but in my heart you're held in chains
And the poetry in my soul
will never let you go.

x°. ☽ °○○°.°○○° ☾ .°x

"I'll hide you in my eyelashes so you're a part of all I see
I'll kiss your soul with all my thoughts and keep you in my poetry."

Michelle Schaper

SOLDIER

I have no need for shiny armour
lacking a dent or bullet hole
I just want your natural lustre
from deep inside your soul
show me all scars of your heart
the sweat and blood
that stain within
I'll give you battles in my bones
etching stories in my skin
you see I fight with my own mind
at times get dragged to war
that's when I need my soldier
to love me so much more.

x°. ꒰ °○°°.°○° ꒱ .°x

"Her heart is her fiercest weapon beating like a newborn savage in her chest as if it could burst straight through her bones never letting her soul rest."

Michelle Schaper

NOBILITY

Her heart is stitched together
with good intentions
her soul is stained
with yesterday's dust
she has had her fair share
of heartache
too many have misused her trust
but she walks
with her head held up high
dressed entirely
in her own strength and passion
she will always shine from inside out
because integrity never goes out of fashion.

x°. ☾ °○∘°.°∘○° ☽ .°x

*"She wears a crown built from her spine of inner strength
and modesty adorned with sparkling jewels to represent
her each and every quality."*

Michelle Schaper

THE LITTLE MERMAID'S TEARS

Storms be raging in the skies
every time a mermaid cries
feeling trapped, not quite whole
dropping tears,
salt of a sirens soul
when oceans stroke your skin
with salty kisses
she will be crying
so you can make your wishes.

x°. ☽ °○○°.°○○° ☾ .°x

[Mermaid Mythology]

The earliest known mermaid legends come from Syria around 1000B.C. where the Syrian goddess Atargatis dove into a lake to take the form of a fish, but the powers there wouldn't allow her to give up her great beauty, so only her bottom half became fish and her top half remained human,

Michelle Schaper

SHIELD of HOPE

When nightfall comes
and your loved ones
have gone to sleep
anxiety wraps itself around you
while all is quiet but your heartbeat
Thoughts appear like little armies
approaching battleground
tiny soldiers lining up
each with new weapons found
One throws doubt your way
another shoots bullets of fear
swords of thoughts
pierce through your mind
causing yet another tear
But somewhere in the darkness
hides your biggest shield of hope
protecting your defences
bringing you new ways to cope
So when your heartbeat softens
and dreaming finally comes your way
may hope hold you
through the night
for you to face another day.

x°. ᧞ °○₀°.°₀○° ℓ .°x

"A new day cupped her heart in its hands as hope wiped away all of her tears."

Michelle Schaper

PEARLS of POETRY

Stars are little kisses
dropped into the night
shimmering like pearls of poetry
upon dark velvet
tiny glowing buttons that appear
when skies are wearing
their evening gowns.

ₓ°. ☽ °○₀°.°○○° ☾ .°ₓ

"One look at you and I began designing stars."

Michelle Schaper

INSTINCT

There is a place
within your soul
of ancient time
and tales of old
where animal spirit
and woman's spirit meet
the wild vitality
rears up to greet
It's a place where
instinct comes to you
so you can recognise
what's true
the place where women
run with wolves to keep
instinctual thoughts
running deep
Run wild through a field
of authentic truth
A woman with her inner wolf.

ₓ°. ☉ °○°˙°○° ℰ .°ₓ

*"Wolves are wild and beautiful, so came the
evolution of women."*

Michelle Schaper

NEVER ENDING STORY

There's a never ending story
hidden in her eyes
if you happen to look deep enough
you'll see some of what she hides
Go beyond the struggles
and the pain
to her very core
she's just been waiting
for the one who'll find
the girl she was before.

x°. ☽ °○°·.°○° ☾ .°x

"Wherever my soul came from is a place my heart longs to find."

Michelle Schaper

GENTLE MEN

He may be a gentleman
but doesn't wear a shirt and tie
he might be sensitive and sweet
even as a tattooed guy
He could be everything at once
gentlest of men, dominant lover
so if you haven't read his stories
don't judge his book by the cover.

x°. ༄ °○°.°○° ༁ .°x

*"He speaks with a tuxedo tongue satin lapelled words
so smooth caressing her mind and weaving a grosgrain
of feelings into her heart."*

Michelle Schaper

PRIMITIVE ART

She never referred to herself
as broken
any fragments of her soul
that had once chipped away
she collected with her scars
and used them as weapons
All the cracks only accentuated
her mosaic heart
to let her light shine through
she wasn't a victim
she was a fucking warrior
she was a shining star
and she was primitive art
wrapped up with skin.

x°. ☾ °○○°.°○○° ☽ .°x

*"She's got that beauty with an edge braveheart,
wild-eyed, classy brutality about her."*

Michelle Schaper

KISSES

I will kiss you everywhere
in the bed, on a chair
I'll kiss you underneath the stars
on each one of your bumpy scars
we'll kiss in the pouring rain
I'll kiss your dreams
and all your pain
I'll kiss you on the table
even on the floor
I'll kiss you in the shower
then I'll kiss you some more
I'll kiss your lips
when demons come to play
I'll kiss every teardrop away
I'll kiss your broken pieces
I will kiss you whole
I'll kiss each corner of your heart
then tenderly kiss your soul.

$_x°. \, \mathfrak{D} \, °\text{o}°°.°°\text{o}° \, \mathfrak{C} \, .°_x$

"Your kiss hits my lips so fiercely I can feel it in my heart."

Michelle Schaper

YOUR SONG

He is the bridge in the music
the lyrics and the tune
he is the voice
the lingering tone
that will make you swoon
He gets stuck in your head
your mind has had him on repeat
for oh, so long
he's the only one you'll dance to
Baby, he's your song.

ₓ°. ☉ °○°°.°○° ☾ .°ₓ

"Since you held me I hear the beat of your heart in every song."

Michelle Schaper

EMPTY ECHOES

Sometimes I wish
for the echoes in the empty
to devour me completely
then I'll no longer
have to listen to the silence
of my heart.

x°. 𝕯 °o∘°.°∘O° ℓ .°x

*"There's a hole in her heart left by the beats that escaped
and you'll hear the echo of a heartbeat
sounding like something she used to feel."*

Michelle Schaper

REBEL ELEGANCE

She has a gypsy glow
and the heart of a wolf
warrior spine -
bulletproof
Stardust in her eyes
witchcraft on her lips
mouth full of love
heaven in her hips
Shining her light
soulful eloquence
a poetic princess -
rebel elegance.

x°. ☽ °○°.°○° ☾ .°x

*"I am not fragile like a heart of glass my fragility is
more like the calm before a storm."*

Michelle Schaper

A FINE LADY

Ride a unicorn
pulling a wagon
to see a fine lady
upon a black dragon
stardust on her fingers
down to the tip of her toes
She shall have magic
wherever she goes.

ₓ°. 𝄐 °○°°.°○° ℭ .°ₓ

"Ride a cock-horse to Bunbury Cross to see a fine lady upon a white horse rings on her fingers and bells on her toes and she shall have music wherever she goes."

- Author Unknown

[The modern rhyme is the best known of a number of verses beginning with the line 'Ride a cock-horse to Bunbury Cross; these include a verse printed in Tommy Thumb's pretty song book]

(c.1744)

Michelle Schaper

RED RIDING HOOD

She wanders through forests
cloaked in her thoughts and dreams
all the colours of Autumn
stitched along the seams
the dusty browns, burnt orange,
mostly rich red
looking as though all the fabric has bled
her heart skips in time
to the beat of the breeze
she rides the wind while it dances
through each of the trees
she came here to find solace
hunting for calm in these woods
becoming one with the earth
this little red riding hood
The universe rises up
offering her its throat
knowing she has the soul of a wolf
breathing under her cloak.

x°. ༄ °○∘°.°∘○° ༄ .°x

'HUNTRESS'
hʌntras/noun
A woman who hunts.
"Artemis goddess of the moon, a virgin and a huntress."

Michelle Schaper

BEAUTY and the BEAST

I let all that I love
crawl under my skin
be it man or sky
earth, saint or sin
I'll always love unconditionally
My heart is a beast
breathing beauty.

x°. ☾ °○○°.°○○° ☽ .°x

*"Please do not speak of allure if you judge by vision
only when you feel with your heart how beauty breathes
I'll know you are beautiful too."*

SENSES CARESSED

I love how you caress
every inch of me
without even touching
all my senses caressed
how your eyes
have me undressed
no one touches me
quite like the way you don't.

ₓ°. ☽ °○○°.°○○° ☾ .°ₓ

*"His whiskey breath on my thighs, my lipstick staining
his skin, he makes love to me with his eyes long before
we make magic of sin."*

Michelle Schaper

WEIRDO

I am the ground below your feet
I am the secret you can't keep
I am the song in your soul deep
I am the teardrop that you weep
I am the promise you won't keep
I am the weirdo to your creep
I am the wolf among the sheep.

x°. ꍉ °o°°.°o° ꍌ .°x

"They tried to morph her heart-shaped soul squeeze her wolf spirit through their own keyhole so she stuffed their sheep- like minds back in the box and threw away all of the locks."

Michelle Schaper

KINGDOM

When you broke me open
and scooped out what's inside
you took most of my heart
stolen secrets, all my pride
but you left behind every sound of blue
dreaming all in ruins
and pieces of you
my heartbeat still drops kisses
even though my heart's not whole
for you'll never extinguish
the fire in my soul
and I won't cut myself
on fragments of you that still remain
(I dance along a razor blades edge
of madness and what's sane)
I'll build a kingdom from the ruins
create a beautiful mosaic
from all the little pieces
you forgot to take.

x°. ☉ °○∘°.°∘○° ☽ .°x

"To get through this thing called life I'll grow with my own truth and feed the highs I will let the wolves inside my heart chew up and spit out any lies."

Michelle Schaper

BLOOM

Everyone has a talent
a skill that is unique
true to their beating heart
each soul its own masterpiece
Some underestimate their worth
they don't seem to recognise
I wish I could let them view their abilities
as seen through my eyes
There's many who seem to hide
behind a shadow of a doubt
through no fault of their own
their voice still growing
loud enough to shout
But you see we're all tiny seeds
there's always room to grow
no matter how many experiences gained
there's never enough wisdom
one could know
So don't compare yourself to others
or feel not good enough
just keep blossoming
beside other seedlings
radiating from each other's love
And don't forget the story

continued

about the daisy and the rose
a flower won't compete
with different types next to it
they just bloom as each one grows.

x°. ☽ °∘°.°∘° ☾ .°x

"Be with those who inspire growth of the soul
if you can't find any, be one who others would want to know."

Michelle Schaper

SWEET POETRY

You see her velutinous petals
then your eyes stop still
she wears her velvety surface well
don't you think it's not a skill
if you look a little closer
you'll glimpse all the thorns she's kept
the words stuck in her throat
reasons why she hasn't slept
And when she bleeds her dreams to life
I wonder if you'll see
hopes and hurts of past and present
hidden in sweet poetry.

ₓ°. ☽ °○∘°.°∘○° ☾ .°ₓ

*"The forces of creation are driven by the impulses of life
to express beauty and truth for everyone."*

Michelle Schaper

RHYTHMIC ART

If you fall in love with me
you must love all the curves
each curl of the letters
making up the words
The ink stains
upon my fingertips
the taste of every verse
that lingers on my lips
All the hidden rhymes
deep inside my heart
the sound of my soul
creating rhythmic art
A realm of elegance
I keep inside of me
the colour of my eyes
a shade of poetry.

ₓ°. ☽ °○∘°.°∘○° ☾ .°ₓ

*"If you want to know her in her entirety
listen to kisses of her heartbeat read her poetry."*

Michelle Schaper

ALWAYS MY HAPPY EVER AFTER

—for my daughters

As a parent I feel I've always given you some
freedom to learn and grow
but I'm more than proud to think I've raised you
to become the woman I now know
You still have that same sensibility
of wonder as when you were my wide-eyed child
I hope you always keep that special spirit rebel
heart and soul so wild
I've watched you gain
your own sense of understanding
while trying to provide a background for your freedom
rendering morals and values as a guide
So my heart bursts with love for you
more and more with each year's passing
every phase you learn and grow through
gaining strength that's everlasting
And even though my heart breaks
when you struggle to comprehend
life's hurts and cruelty
those are the times your kindness shines
and the world pales in comparison to your beauty.

x°. ☽ °○°°.°○° ☾ .°x

*"May all our daughters be divinely blessed
and recognise their inner goddess."*

Michelle Schaper

FUCK CANCER

—for my MockingJay

It's time to put to sleep
any bad blood,
is no longer mine to keep
I'll turn the poison into stardust
focusing on my dreams
I'm growing Warrior Wings
while kicking this disease
I will put up a fight
keep my heart filled up with wishes
so if someday you see
my heartbeat's run out of kisses
Know I tried with all I am
to reclaim what Cancer stole
and you will always find my spirit
sleeping safe inside your soul.

ₓ°. ☉ °○∘°.°∘○° ℓ .°ₓ

*"A MockingJay symbolises a creature with a spirit of its own
MockingJays are fictional hybrid creatures that have broken free
from control. These birds are signs of resistance and rebellion."*

AUTHOR'S NOTE

Some of the most beautiful people I know struggle daily with illness, mental health issues, grief, debilitating disease and heartbreak. These thoughts from my heart are for all warriors who find their strength to cope with life and still manage to empower others along their way. I wish for my words to be a blanket of hope to provide comfort while offering a hint of romance and mischief at the same time.

ₓ°. ☽ °○°°.°○° ☾ .°ₓ

"When your heartbeat softens and dreaming finally comes your way, May hope hold you through the night, for you to face another day."

—Michelle Schaper

ABOUT THE AUTHOR

Michelle Schaper, from Western Australia, works as a support worker/carer for disabilities, (or as she says, 'enhancing people's abilities.') She is a mentor/advocate for mental health and domestic violence and has written poetry since her childhood. You'll find more of Michelle's work on Facebook at facebook.com/chellessoulpoems and @michellesoulkissing on Instagram.

www.ingramcontent.com/pod-product-compliance
Lightning Source LLC
Chambersburg PA
CBHW071021120626
46546CB00003B/1190